THE CATCHER IN THE RYE ENIGMA

J.D. Salinger's Mind Control Triggering Device
or a
Coincidental Literary Obsession of Criminals?

THE UNDERGROUND KNOWLEDGE SERIES

James&Lance
MORCAN

THE CATCHER IN THE RYE ENIGMA:
J.D. Salinger's Mind Control Triggering Device or a Coincidental
Literary Obsession of Criminals?

Published by:
Sterling Gate Books
78 Pacific View Rd,
Papamoa 3118,
Bay of Plenty,
New Zealand
sterlinggatebooks@gmail.com

Special Note: This title is an extended version of Chapters 27, 2, 12, 21 & 23 of *The Orphan Conspiracies: 29 Conspiracy Theories from The Orphan Trilogy* (Sterling Gate Books, 2014) by James Morcan & Lance Morcan. This title therefore contains a combination of new material as well as recycled material (in many cases verbatim excerpts) from *The Orphan Conspiracies*.

National Library of New Zealand publication data:

Morcan, James 1978-
Morcan, Lance 1948-
Title: The Catcher in the Rye Enigma
Edition: First ed.
Format: Paperback
Publisher: Sterling Gate Books
ISBN: 978-0-473-38049-6

CONTENTS

INTRODUCTION

The 1951 novel *The Catcher in the Rye,* by J.D. Salinger, is arguably the most controversial book of all time.

Nicknamed the 'Bible of teenage angst,' the classic novel, which is frequently labeled immoral by different groups, has been banned in various parts of America over the decades. From 1961–1982 it was the most censored book in libraries and high schools across the United States. School principals have branded it communist propaganda and teachers have been fired for assigning it to students.

However, the main controversy, and indeed the most common reason for it being banned,

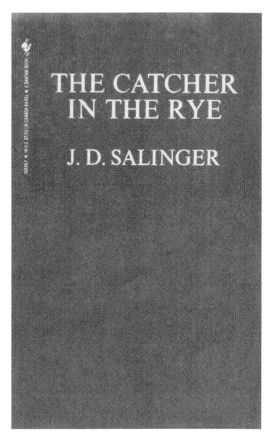

Above: The Catcher in the Rye cover from the 1985 Bantam edition.

"Catcher-in-the-rye-red-cover" by Bantam
Photo shot by Derek Jensen (Tysto), January 14, 2006.
Licensed under Public Domain via Wikimedia Commons

was that it either directly inspired or was associated with some of the most infamous crimes of the 20th Century.

Presidential assassins and would-be Presidential assassins, stalkers and murderers of film stars and music icons are among the known deranged individuals who were obsessed with Salinger's book—a book which many claim to be an assassination trigger device.

The murderers, stalkers and their victims and targets, who are all either confirmed or rumored to be part of the *The Catcher in the Rye* mystery, include John Lennon, Ronald Reagan, Robert John Bardo, Lee Harvey Oswald, Bobby Kennedy, Madonna, Martin Luther King, Mark David Chapman, Jack Ruby, Rebecca Schaeffer, Jodie Foster, JFK, John Hinckley Junior, James Earl Ray and Sirhan Sirhan.

The allegation pointed at Salinger is that he craftily implanted into the book coded messages that act as post-hypnotic suggestions or mind control triggers. In turn, these enabled CIA handlers to activate Manchurian Candidates for planned assassinations.

Many believe the novel was part of the CIA's extensive mind control program known as *MK-Ultra,* and that while assassins, or future assassins, were being brainwashed they were forced to read the book over and over until it was embedded in their minds.

These ideas and others have been covered in pop culture, especially in the 1997 film *Conspiracy Theory,* in which Mel Gibson's character carries a copy of Salinger's book with him at all times. The cleverly-written film, which at first appears to be nothing but a lightweight romantic comedy co-starring rom-com queen Julia Roberts, becomes more intense as the story progresses and it's revealed Mel Gibson's character is entwined with the CIA and is a mind control victim of the agency's MK-Ultra program.

Season three of the TV series *Criminal Minds* features an episode called *Limelight* in which the character of David Rossi, played by Joe Mantegna, mentions having once interviewed serial killer Ted Bundy who told him, "If you wanna stop people from becoming like me, don't burn Catcher in the Rye."

An episode of the animated TV series *South Park* also covers the mind control theory in a humorous way when one of the show's young characters reads the book then picks up a knife and starts saying, "Kill John Lennon, kill John Lennon." The boy is disappointed when his

Above: A painting of J.D. Salinger

"Portrait of JD Salinger" by User:StefanoRR
Own work (original model: Salinger's military college yearbook).
Licensed under Public Domain via Wikimedia Commons

father informs him the former Beatle was assassinated years earlier.

But seriously, can *The Catcher in the Rye* really wake MK-Ultra *sleeper assassins* from their slumber?

That's up to you, the reader, to decide by the end of this book.

It must be noted the idea that assassination codes are buried deep in Salinger's book is one of the oldest conspiracy theories around and has often been explored over the decades. In fact, many readers familiar with *Catcher* conspiracies may think all the theories have already been proven to be false and there's no need to drag them up yet again.

However, given what we've unearthed in our research for this book and indeed the entirety of *The Underground Knowledge Series*— especially the unique revelations on the history of mind control, the effectiveness of subliminal messages, the latest scientific studies on the brain, the Americanized Nazis in *Project Paperclip* and the recently declassified documents on real-life Manchurian Candidates—we believe some of the theories swirling about Salinger's classic deserve another look.

James Morcan & Lance Morcan

1

A History of Mind Control

"Anyway, I keep picturing all these little kids playing some game in this big field of rye and all. Thousands of little kids, and nobody's around—nobody big, I mean—except me. And I'm standing on the edge of some crazy cliff. What I have to do, I have to catch everybody if they start to go over the cliff—I mean if they're running and they don't look where they're going I have to come out from somewhere and catch them. That's all I do all day. I'd just be the catcher in the rye and all. I know it's crazy, but that's the only thing I'd really like to be."

–J.D. Salinger, *The Catcher in the Rye*

Before detailing the various crimes and overall mysteries surrounding J.D. Salinger's classic novel itself, there are three underreported or little-known subjects we must cover first. These are all crucial pieces of the puzzle, necessary (as a bare minimum) for any person to make an informed decision as to whether they think *The Catcher in the Rye* is a "Mind Control Triggering Device" or simply a "Coincidental Literary Obsession of Criminals" as per this book's subtitle.

The first of these three necessary ingredients is the secret history of mind control . . .

Manipulating the thoughts and behaviour of unsuspecting victims has been occurring for at least 60 years. From declassified files from governments, intelligence agencies and the military, to media reports and scientific journals, to interviews with psychiatrists involved in experiments, mind control is on-the-record and official.

It's worth considering here what British author and pacifist Aldous Huxley wrote in his 1958 non-fiction work *Brave New World Revisited:* "It is perfectly possible for a man to be out of prison, and yet not free—to be under no physical constraint and yet to be a psychological captive, compelled to think, feel

Above: Aldous Huxley warned the public
about mind control.

*"Aldous Huxley" by Not given – Transferred from tr.wikipedia.
Licensed under Public Domain via Wikimedia Commons*

and act as the representatives of the national state, or of some private interest within the nation, wants him to think, feel and act."

Huxley was alluding to the dark art of mind control, suggesting who the architects of this malicious behavior modification were and implying its extensive possibilities.

During the course of conducting research for this book and several of our other titles, we uncovered the little known history of mind control, and it's something of a long, spooky rabbit hole to say the least. By reading and analyzing court cases, doctors' reports and declassified documents, we became aware of the often disastrous impact mind control programs have had on the lives of innocent civilians over the decades.

MIND CONTROL IN THE THIRD REICH

Most of the earliest reports of mind control come from Nazi Germany. In fact, many researchers have surmised that all subsequent mind control programs—including British, Russian and American programs—have firm roots in these early German experiments and applications.

"Hitler's philosophy and his concept of man in general were shaped to a decisive degree by psychiatry," according to Dr. Thomas Roeder and his co-authors Volker Kubillus and Anthony Burwell in their 1995 book *Psychiatrists: The Men Behind Hitler*. They wrote: "An influential cluster of psychiatrists and their frightening theories and methods collectively form the missing piece of the puzzle of Hitler, the Third Reich, the atrocities and their dreadful legacy."

SS officer Doctor Josef Mengele, infamously nicknamed the *Angel of Death* for his horrific human experiments at Auschwitz, is said to have been employed in the *Lebensborn* program (an SS program devised to propagate Aryan traits in children), albeit quite secretively.

Doctor Mengele conducted one of the earliest studies on trauma-based mind control during his tenure at the Auschwitz concentration camp. Some researchers say that the Angel of Death's mind control methodologies became the primary brainwashing techniques used to reprogram the young children in *Lebensborn* facilities Europe-wide.

These advances in mind control techniques and technologies didn't disappear with the fall of Nazi Germany. When the Soviets and the Americans invaded the country and divided the

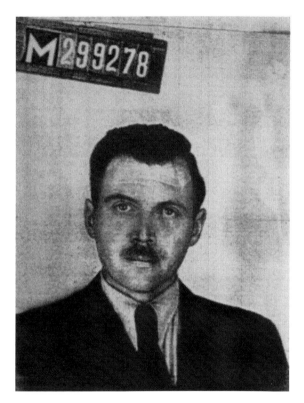

Above: German SS officer, Josef Mengele.
(Argentina, 1956).

*"WP Josef Mengele 1956" by Anonymous photographer
Gerald Astor: "The last Nazi – The Life and Times of Dr. Josef
Mengele, p. 206. D.I. Fine, 1985.
Licensed under Public Domain via Wikimedia Commons*

spoils, they both inherited these sophisticated mind control breakthroughs.

In Chapter 6 you will read about J.D. Salinger's wartime relations with Nazis and the connection this *may* have to potential hidden mind control programming in *The Catcher in the Rye*.

BLUEBIRD

Project Bluebird was the CIA's first official behavior modification program. Created in 1949, its purpose was to study behavior modification, interrogation and general mind control as well as interrelated subjects.

Bluebird was an umbrella project spawned from the US Government's super-secret *Project Paperclip*. Also known as *Operation Paperclip*, it was a sinister venture that brought hundreds of Nazi scientists to America immediately after World War Two. They were spirited into the US, often with new identities. Many were experts in brainwashing and other mind control methods. Some were even known war criminals, prosecuted during the Nuremberg Trials.

Yes you read that right: the US Government's mind control programs stem directly from the horrendous psychiatric experiments the Nazis conducted during the Holocaust.

Again, this may all sound very far-fetched, but we implore you to do the research if you can't believe it. Paperclip is on-the-record, and fascist methodologies really did worm their way into nations throughout the West. (See chapter 2 for a detailed history of Project Paperclip).

ARTICHOKE

By 1950 (a year before *The Catcher in the Rye* was first published), Project Bluebird had morphed into *Project Artichoke,* which was a forerunner to the better known *Project MK-Ultra.* Artichoke included non-consensual medical experiments in which elite psychiatrists created new identities in some people, amnesia in others and inserted false memories into the minds of the remaining subjects.

Professional magician John Mulholland was quietly recruited by Artichoke administrators to hypnotize subjects and prepare them for mind control experiments. In the early 1950's, he stopped performing magic shows, citing health problems. However, it was later revealed Mulholland had actually become an intelligence agent for the Central Intelligence Agency.

The following excerpt from a now declassified CIA memo dated 1952 summarizes the agency's motivations with Artichoke: "Can we get control of an individual to the point where he will do our bidding against his will and even against fundamental laws of nature, such as self-preservation?"

MK-Ultra

The most documented government mind control program worldwide is Project MK-Ultra. This human research operation in behavioral engineering began in the early 1950's and was run through the CIA's Scientific Intelligence Division. It continued for a quarter of a century, and it used American and Canadian citizens as its test subjects, usually without their knowledge or consent.

Doctor Sidney Gottlieb was in charge of MK-Ultra from its inception until the mid-1960's. By all accounts a callous and eccentric individual, Gottlieb was the inspiration for Peter Sellers' title role in Stanley Kubrick's 1964 black comedy *Dr. Strangelove*.

Many researchers have deduced that the CIA's goal was to create real-life Manchurian Candidates. We'd have to agree, although there are probably wider applications of effective mind control than producing programmed assassins.

As a result of the United States' Freedom of Information Act, tens of thousands of government documents relating to Project MK-Ultra have been obtained by independent researchers. Other documents regarding MK-Ultra have also been officially declassified.

The project finally came to the American public's attention in 1975 when it was discussed in the US Congress.

President Gerald Ford also set up a commission to investigate MK-Ultra and other CIA activities. This led to Senate hearings on MK-Ultra in 1977 during which Senator Ted Kennedy stated: "The Deputy Director of the CIA revealed that over 30 universities and institutions were involved in an extensive testing and experimentation program which included covert drug tests on unwitting citizens at all social levels, high and low, native Americans and foreign."

Seemingly following the same mind control protocols laid down by the Nazis, the CIA selected people from the most vulnerable sectors of American society to experiment on— orphans, the mentally ill, prisoners, the poor, the handicapped. Basically those who didn't have a voice or the wherewithal to seek help.

CIA doctors involved in MK-Ultra experiments incorporated various methods to manipulate people's brains and alter their mental states. These included disruptive electromagnetic signals, sensory deprivation, hypnosis, electroshock, sexual abuse and drugs, especially LSD.

"In 1953, Allen Dulles, then director of the USA Central Intelligence Agency (CIA), named Dr Sidney Gottlieb to direct the CIA's MKULTRA programme, which included experiments conducted by psychiatrists to create amnesia, new dissociated identities, new memories, and responses to hypnotic access codes. In 1972, then-CIA director Richard Helms and Gottlieb ordered the destruction of all MKULTRA records. A clerical error spared seven boxes, containing 1738 documents, over 17,000 pages. This archive was declassified through a Freedom of Information Act Request in 1977, though the names of most people, universities, and hospitals are redacted ... The United States Senate held a hearing exposing the abuses of MKULTRA, entitled "Project MKULTRA, the CIA's program of research into behavioral modification" (1977)."

—Orit Badouk Epstein, *Ritual Abuse and Mind Control: The Manipulation of Attachment Needs*

Equally disturbing, the list of infamous people connected to, or rumored to be associated with, MK-Ultra almost reads like a who's who of the worst American criminals in the 20th Century.

Lawrence Teeter, the lawyer representing Robert F. Kennedy's assassin, Sirhan Sirhan, proposed that his client was an MK-Ultra victim. Teeter stated Sirhan displayed all the signs of being hypnotized before and after RFK's assassination.

Enough evidence exists to conclude that Theodore Kaczynski, otherwise known as the Unabomber, participated in MK-Ultra experiments conducted at Harvard University from 1959 to 1962. Although these Harvard experiments appeared relatively benign, they were surreptitiously sponsored by the CIA and that seems tantamount to a smoking gun.

Oklahoma City bomber Timothy McVeigh—a decorated Gulf War veteran—claimed to have been implanted with some kind of microchip while serving in the US Army. He also claimed he was yet another victim of MK-Ultra's vast web.

Interestingly, the US Army Major and mind control victim that Denzel Washington played in the 2004 remake of *The Manchurian*

Candidate also had a microchip implanted in his body. Perhaps in a case of art imitating life, Washington's character was also a decorated Gulf War veteran who served in *Operation Desert Storm,* just as McVeigh did.

The 1978 Jonestown massacre in the jungles of Guyana is considered by various independent investigators to have been a large scale MK-Ultra experiment. Until 9/11, the Jonestown tragedy had the dubious distinction of being the greatest loss of American civilian lives in one single act.

There are also possible MK-Ultra links to Ronald Reagan's would-be assassin John Hinckley, Jr., as well as John Lennon's killer Mark David Chapman. Suspiciously, a copy of *The Catcher in the Rye* was found on both men upon their arrest—suspicious as J.D. Salinger's classic novel is said by many to be a mind control trigger device for MK-Ultra victims.

In 1976, more than two decades after MK-Ultra began, President Gerald Ford prohibited "experimentation with drugs on human subjects, except with the informed consent, in writing and witnessed by a disinterested party, of each such human subject."

However, repeated rumors suggest the MK-Ultra program continues—probably under

Above: FBI mugshot of Timothy McVeigh.

"McVeigh mugshot" by FBI Lab forensic artist
A_McVeigh_sketch_and_pic.jpg.
Licensed under Public Domain via Wikimedia Commons

another codename and perhaps as a Black Op rather than a government-sanctioned project.

At the civilian level, more MK-Ultra victims continue to come forward. In 1995, there were new US congressional hearings on MK-Ultra, which included statements made by mind control victims and the therapists who treated them.

"There have been extensive human rights violations by American psychiatrists over the last 70 years. These doctors were paid by the American taxpayer through CIA and military contracts. It is past time for these abuses to stop, it is past time for a reckoning, and it is past time for individual doctors to be held accountable. The Manchurian Candidate Programs are of much more than "historical" interest. ARTICHOKE, BLUEBIRD, MKULTRA and MKSEARCH are precursors of mind control programs that are operational in the twenty first century. Human rights violations by psychiatrists must be ongoing in programs like COPPER GREEN, the interrogation program at Abu Ghraib prison in Iraq."

–Colin A. Ross, The C.I.A. Doctors: Human Rights Violations by American Psychiatrists

2

AMERICANIZED NAZIS

The second crucial piece of the puzzle that needs to be comprehended before making an informed judgement on whether or not *Catcher* and Salinger were just coincidentally associated with so many separate crimes, is what went down at the end of, and immediately following, WW2. Specifically between the US and Germany.

"What national security permits the removal of fundamental power from the hands of the American people and validates the ascendancy of an invisible government in the United States? That kind of national security, gentlemen of the jury, is when it smells like it, feels like it, and looks like it, you call it what it is: Fascism!"

—Monologue delivered by Kevin Costner and written by Oliver Stone in JFK (1991)

History reminds us that communism was already a dominant political force even before the echoes of World War Two had faded. After the war, as the Soviet Union began to encroach on more and more nations, communism and the threat of nuclear war were the West's two big fears.

However, there is a lesser known school of thought that says fascism actually posed an even bigger threat post-WW2.

On the surface, this theory doesn't make much sense for officially speaking fascism was all but expunged from the Earth when the Allies demolished the Nazi war machine. From then on, the only fascist remnants appeared to be obscure far-right political parties as well as the odd white supremacist or anti-Semitic group.

But that's just on the surface and what the history books tell us.

Alternative versions that lie beneath commonly accepted 20th Century history claim many Western nations—the US in particular—only missed out on becoming fascist states by a whisker. Such ideas pose the almost unthinkable question: what if Nazism morphed into something else and continued underground, in another guise, in the West?

Fascist ideologies, practices and technologies didn't vanish with the death of Hitler and Nazi Germany, this radical conspiracy theory suggests. Instead, they actually *grew* in popularity with fascist supporters springing up in senior positions of power in various Western governments. However, this theory asserts that fascism became harder to detect because of its more subtle implementation, which perhaps indicates this new breed of fascists learnt from the failures of the Third Reich.

Sounds ridiculous, doesn't it?

We thought so too . . . until we came across a little known US Government program whose declassified files reveal damning evidence of co-operation between Nazi party survivors and the highest ranking American politicians.

PROJECT PAPERCLIP

As stated in chapter 1, America's mind control programs stemmed from the US Government's *Project Paperclip,* but it wasn't just Nazi brainwashing techniques the Americans inherited. They also seized Nazi scientists whose number included known war criminals.

The top secret project, also known as *Operation Paperclip,* was a nefarious undertaking that allowed Nazi scientists to migrate to the US without prosecution. Some had studied brainwashing and other mind control methods first-hand in the concentration camps; many were rocket scientists who had been directly involved in the development of Germany's feared V-1 and V-2 rockets. The latter's contribution would pave the way for NASA and the Moon landings, and also for America's Intercontinental Ballistic Missile program.

Project Paperclip was as much about denying German scientific expertise to the Soviet Union and Britain as it was benefiting US science, defence and space programs. This was happening as the Cold War loomed don't forget and an uncertain world was being carved up by superpowers. It was a three-way grab (for the spoils) between the Americans, the Soviets and the Brits.

Remember, Nazi Germany's scientific breakthroughs were nothing short of revolutionary. Although it didn't last long, the Nazi era was arguably the most accelerated scientific period in history, especially when suppressed or little known Nazi inventions are taken into account. History reminds us how easily the Third Reich dominated Europe despite being greatly outnumbered by the combined Allied forces. The Germans ruled the land, sea and air, and it was obvious to all they had superior technologies.

The Allies learned the hard way that Nazi engineers and scientists had made incredible breakthroughs in various fields. These included semi-conductors, plasma physics, ballistic missiles, laser technologies, electromagnetic weapons, computers, astrophysics, infrared night vision and miniature electronics to name but a few. While some of these breakthroughs were commonly known, others remained classified and were kept secret for decades.

A *BBC News* report dated November 21, 2005 nicely summarizes the situation that existed at the close of WW2. That report states: "The end of World War II saw an intense scramble for Nazi Germany's many technological secrets. The Allies vied to plunder as much equipment and expertise as possible from the rubble of the Thousand Year Reich for themselves, while preventing others from doing the same."

The report continues: "The range of Germany's technical achievement astounded Allied scientific intelligence experts accompanying the invading forces in 1945."

That *BBC News* report also reminds us "It was the US and the Soviet Union which, in the first days of the Cold War, found themselves in a race against time to uncover Hitler's scientific secrets."

Project Paperclip was America's solution to this problem. Supposedly named after the paperclips that were used to attach the files of the recruited German scientists, the project was the brainchild of America's Joint Intelligence Objectives Agency (JOIA), a sub-committee of the Joint Chief's of Staff of the US Armed Forces.

Project Paperclip's architects viewed their secret endeavor as the solution to harnessing Nazi scientists' superior knowledge and expertise, and positioning America as the world leader in science and technology.

Above: A group of 104 German Rocket
scientists in Texas.

"Project Paperclip Team at Fort Bliss"
Image by NASA under Photo ID: NIX MSFC-8915531
Licensed under Public Domain via Wikimedia Commons

PAPERCLIP NAZIS GET THEIR GREENCARDS

The recruitment of Nazi scientists began as soon as the war ended although the project itself wasn't officially signed off by President Harry Truman until three months later.

It should be noted that while Truman stipulated that scientists who were active in the Nazi Party, or who actively supported it, should not be recruited, such limitations would have precluded the recruitment of the most eligible prospects.

Declassified files show that Truman's orders were ignored. All recruits were cleared to work in America after their backgrounds were *cleaned up*. US authorities created fake resumes, removing any mention of Nazi involvement, and entire false identities were designed for the highest profile war criminals.

Those same declassified files also indicate that, at one point, around 10,000 Nazis were living undercover in America. (Some estimates are as high as 15,000). Many were awarded citizenship. Imagine how many descendants of those Nazis reside in the US today. It's quite possible some are reading this book right now.

Tom Bower's 1987 book, *The Paperclip Conspiracy: The Hunt for the Nazi Scientists,* provides an insightful look at the history behind the project and reminds readers how quickly morals can be set to one side to meet an apparent need—in this case the need for scientific knowledge. The author cites official WW2 files as his main source of information.

Reviewers of Bower's book have picked up on a key point he makes—notably that the Americans, Soviets and Brits were fiercely competing to secure Nazi scientists for themselves and were prepared to overlook the fact some, or possibly many, were known war criminals.

And of course, those Nazi war criminals included some doctors involved with mind control experiments and therefore later influenced official US mind control operations such as Artichoke, Bluebird and MK-Ultra. The latter being the program that conspiracy theorists believe *The Catcher in the Rye* was somehow a part of or else intimately associated with.

WELCOME MAT ROLLED OUT FOR WAR CRIMINALS

In the post-war years in the US, Project Paperclip remained hush-hush and only a select few knew of its existence. It wasn't until much later the American public learned the truth—or part of the truth at least.

A US Justice Department report dated December 2006 states: "In the 1970's, the public was shocked to learn that some Nazi persecutors had emigrated to the United States. There were calls for their expulsion and legislation was passed to facilitate their deportation. OSI (the Office of Special Investigations) was created in 1979 to handle the caseload."

In the report, the Justice Department goes to great lengths to explain that the obstacles to success in prosecuting these Nazi war criminals were formidable. It lists numerous reasons supporting this opinion—not the least being that so much time had passed and many of the recruits had died.

Several prominent US newspapers have claimed that the Justice Department report reveals OSI investigators learned some of the Nazis were knowingly granted entry to the US even though government officials were aware of their pasts. Some journalists have observed that America, with its proud history of providing sanctuary for the persecuted including Holocaust survivors, had ended up giving asylum to some of their persecutors.

A *New York Times* article dated November 13, 2010 takes the Justice Department to task for sitting on its report for so long. The article states: "The 600-page report, which the Justice Department has tried to keep secret for four years, provides new evidence about more than two dozen of the most notorious Nazi cases of the last three decades."

However, it's the article's intro that caught our eye. It reads: "A secret history of the US Government's Nazi-hunting operation concludes that American intelligence officials created a safe haven in the US for Nazis and their collaborators after WW2 and it details decades of clashes, often hidden, with other nations over war criminals here and abroad."

While over 300 Nazi migrants have either been deported or refused visas to America since OSI's formation, the Justice Department's report leaves no doubt the US Government collaborated with notorious war criminals and knowingly granted them entry into the US.

The CIA doesn't escape censure either. Its "use of Nazis for postwar intelligence purposes" comes under the spotlight in the report.

Given that mind control as we know it was first mastered during Hitler's reign, it's no surprise Nazi psychiatrists were also among those brought into the US post WW2.

As Dr. Thomas Roeder and co-authors Volker Kubillus and Anthony Burwell revealed in their 1995 book *Psychiatrists: The Men Behind Hitler,* psychiatry was highly valued in the Third Reich. From declassified Paperclip files it's obvious the science of the mind was equally valued by US authorities.

What's insane is that after the American public had paid an enormously high price to win WW2, US taxpayers then paid for Josef Mengele's protégés to live and work in America.

This means that Doctor Mengele's dark scientific legacy not only included the countless victims of the Holocaust experiments he conducted, but also the thousands of American and Canadian casualties of the MK-Ultra program.

When considering Project Paperclip's influence on modern mind control programs, the doctor's moniker *The Angel of Death* suddenly becomes even more relevant.

3

REAL-LIFE MANCHURIAN
CANDIDATES

"His brain has not only been washed, as they say. It has been dry cleaned."

—The Manchurian Candidate (1962 feature film)

The third and final piece of "underground knowledge" required to accurately unravel the mystery surrounding *The Catcher in the Rye* is the evidence to support the existence of *real* Manchurian Candidates . . .

In 1959, Richard Condon's classic psychological thriller *The Manchurian Candidate* was published. The book's plot revolves around the son of a leading American political family being brainwashed into becoming a communist assassin without his knowledge or consent.

Ever since then, the title has become a catch-phrase amongst conspiracy theorists who swear they've got *evidence* to prove governments around the world have such mind-controlled assassins at their disposal.

They often list the likes of Lee Harvey Oswald, Sirhan Sirhan, Jack Ruby, Mark David Chapman and James Earl Ray as being likely Manchurian Candidates; and they point out that nearly all these men, as well as numerous other infamous lone gunmen, claimed after being captured that they were patsies who were being mind-controlled.

However, the reality is programmed killers only exist in the realms of fictional stories and in the warped minds of those wearing tinfoil hats. There is no hard evidence to confirm the existence of Manchurian Candidates.

At least that's what the authorities would have us believe.

MK = MIND KONTROL

The concept of creating brainwashed assassins with the help of J.D. Salinger's book or otherwise could accurately be described as being very far-fetched, were it not for one thing: the officially acknowledged, real-life MK-Ultra program.

To recap, *Project MK-Ultra,* the most documented government mind control program uncovered yet, began in the early 1950's, using unwitting American and Canadian citizens as its test subjects. We know this as a result of the many thousands of US Government documents that have been publicly accessed courtesy of the Freedom of Information Act, and the release of other formerly classified documents relating to MK-Ultra.

These revelations generated considerable publicity, debate, research—both official and unofficial—and a number of feature films, documentaries and television series.

Then there are the rumored Manchurian Candidates said to have been brainwashed by US Military factions, with heavy CIA involvement, to carry out assassinations or other such acts for those who have programmed them.

Incidentally, the best description we've found of a Manchurian Candidate is someone with an artificially created multiple personality; that personality has various identities; if one identity performs an act and gets caught, another identity takes over and the original identity has no recollection of the act he (seems it's always a man) committed, so the information remains hidden from interrogators.

Mind control expert and award-winning author Dr. Alan Scheflin has for years claimed that, thanks to the CIA, MK-Ultra is still alive and well in America and that declassified documents show the CIA is creating a new kind of weapon. Scheflin, whose books include *The Mind Manipulators,* leaves little doubt the *weapon* he refers to is a Manchurian Candidate and, he says, such people aren't responsible for their actions because they're being controlled.

Scheflin's assertions are confirmed by renowned psychiatrist Dr. Colin A. Ross, president and founder of the Colin A. Ross Institute for Psychological Trauma, who says he used the Freedom of Information Act to source US Government documents that show the CIA and different branches of the military continue to be active in the mind control business.

This revelation contradicts the US Government's official statements which say there have been no further mind control programs since MK-Ultra was shut down in 1973.

Dr. Ross likens the selection of Manchurian Candidates to the selection process for the military's documented radiation and germ warfare experiments that were conducted on soldiers who were always unaware of the dangers involved. He says the declassified documents he has sourced on mind control experiments reveal volunteers received huge amounts of electric shocks, which permanently wiped out their memories.

"This fall I think you're riding for—it's a special kind of fall, a horrible kind. The man falling isn't permitted to feel or hear himself hit bottom. He just keeps falling and falling."

–J.D. Salinger, The Catcher in the Rye

MIND GAMES

Assassins experiencing amnesia is a subject that's been explored in various bestselling novels and blockbuster movies, including

Robert Ludlum's *Bourne* novels and subsequent film adaptations.

In the 2007 feature film *The Bourne Ultimatum,* which stars Matt Damon and was directed by Paul Greengrass, a surprise twist delivered via flashbacks in the film's third act reveals that Jason Bourne had actually volunteered to become an assassin. These flashbacks show Bourne has had his identity fractured and his memories erased after having been put through a series of trauma-based psychological trials that eventually broke down his original personality.

Such works of fiction are clearly inspired by conspiracy theories which insist this is how mind-controlled assassins are created.

Numerous sources—some reliable, some not—report that Manchurian Candidates are subjected to receiving large amounts of LSD and other drugs, isolation, interrogation, hypnotism, and food and sleep deprivation as well as electric shocks. It seems trauma-based torture is used to program inductees and to promote the development of alternate psyches, or personalities, which would enable them to function *normally* and then to kill on command but have no recollection of their actions.

This fracturing of the psyche is said to be conducive to creating the phenomenon that has been termed *sleeper assassins.*

According to such theories, the first psychiatrists employed to master mind control studied mental patients who had been diagnosed with Multiple Personality Disorder, which medical science has since renamed Dissociative Identity Disorder. Many of those psychiatrists are said to have been Paperclip Nazi doctors who were brought to the US after conducting radical psychiatric experiments on patients during the Holocaust—the same doctors whose victims not only included Jews, Gyspies, political agitators and homosexuals, but also the mentally ill.

"The victim of mind-manipulation does not know that he is a victim."

—Aldous Huxley, excerpt from his 1958 non-fiction book Brave New World Revisited.

Above: Disabled Jewish prisoners at the Buchenwald
concentration camp.

"Buchenwald Disabled Jews 13132 crop."
Licensed under Public Domain via Wikimedia Commons

DOCUMENTED CIA SLEEPER ASSASSINS

On December 2, 2010, *Russia Today* ran an article headed *CIA creating real life Manchurian Candidates?* The news outlet's report details the statements of a group of US military veterans who claimed their government had created sleeper assassins long ago. Decades ago in fact.

The vets were quoted as saying that from 1950 until 1975 experiments on themselves and other US soldiers were conducted at the Army's Edgewood Arsenal in Maryland where "the government messed with their minds, implanted microchips and electrodes" during "mind control experiments."

"They are alleging," the article continues, "top secret CIA, military and even university scientists experimented on them with the purpose of implanting remote control devices in their brains to eventually turn them into robot-like assassins."

Documents, which according to the article include declassified research papers from the Office of Naval Research as well as results of experiments conducted at Harvard and Yale, show how hypnosis and electro-implant experiments were first conducted on animals.

This involved inserting electrodes into the brains of dolphins, cats and dogs. By all accounts, the tests were a success in that the scientists conducting them were able to control the actions of the laboratory animals via remote transmitters.

The next stage of testing was on humans— volunteers who apparently weren't clear about what they were letting themselves in for—and proved equally successful. The individuals were mind controlled via the electrode brain implants and carried out a range of actions that signals beamed to their brains instructed them to do.

In what's likely to be a case of art imitating life, the electrode implants used, on the record, by the US Government for brainwashing soldiers echoes the 2004 remake of *The Manchurian Candidate* starring Denzel Washington and Liev Schreiber. In that film, Schreiber's character has electrodes implanted in his brain by neuroscientists.

The aforementioned mind control expert Dr. Colin A. Ross says the account of the US military veterans who were experimented on, as well as the official government documents detailing the experiments, all prove "this is absolutely documented fact."

"People can be in a sleeper state indefinably," Dr. Ross adds, "but of course this is all secret and classified."

Although more recent mind control science remains classified, creating sleeper assassins all sounds very possible given what is known to have occurred during MK-Ultra. In fact, it not only sounds possible, but highly likely. After all, if the long-desired Manchurian Candidate phenomenon was proven to be a reality decades ago, something tells us senior intelligence agents wouldn't just say to each other, "Oh well, we proved it's possible, but we won't send any mind controlled assassins out into the field as that would be immoral."

According to our research, it's very probable sleeper assassins are in existence all over the world today, quietly carrying out *hits* for the global elite. Given mind control has been a documented fact for well over half a century, the powers that be must surely now have all the science needed to create as many brainwashed assassins as they require.

"Years ago I worked for the CIA on the MK ULTRA program. Are you familiar with it? It was mind control. "Manchurian Candidate" kind of stuff. That's a vulgar generalization. But

yes, you take an ordinary man and turn him into an assassin. That was our goal."

*–Brian Helgeland (screenwriter of) Conspiracy
Theory (1997)*

THE GOVERNOR TO THE RESCUE

Perhaps the most high profile investigation into MK-Ultra and mind controlled operatives has been conducted by Jesse Ventura, former Governor of Minnesota, who is probably America's—and possibly the world's—best known conspiracy theorist.

The Governor fronts *Sleeper Assassins,* a 2010 episode of the popular US television series *Conspiracy Theory with Jesse Ventura.* In the episode, he and his team of investigators present a fairly compelling case that Manchurian Candidates in the form of programmed killers do exist in present-day America.

Ventura, who by dearth of his political status and former career in the US Navy had—and to an extent still has—access to official documents, facilities and personnel at the highest levels, informs his audience the US military has been experimenting with mind control since the 1950's.

Jesse Ventura—Sleeper Assassins starts with Ventura telling viewers he has uncovered a Government plot to turn ordinary citizens into programmed killers.

"I've also seen how hypnosis, torture and other techniques can make ordinary people do things they otherwise couldn't do," he says. "I met a man who says they did it to him. All the high-profile assassins who fit this same pattern . . . believe the government turned them into weapons. Could this be a coincidence? I don't think so."

The most intriguing point of the episode is when Ventura interviews whistleblower Robert Duncan O'Finioan, a self-professed former Manchurian Candidate who candidly reveals the methods used to *take over* his mind and reveals the types of missions he undertook whilst under the influence of mind control.

O'Finioan, who is said to have unusual body strength, martial arts talents and alter egos that can be triggered, also claims he and others like him were "taken" and "genetically enhanced with implants" and "turned into something more than a normal human being"—so they almost literally became fighting machines.

O'Finioan appears to be the go-to guy for any conspiracy theorist wanting to add credibility to his or her theory on Manchurian Candidates. He shows up on numerous websites and, it appears, he was and maybe still is the subject of at least one planned book and film.

An item dated January 2007 on the popular ProjectCamelot.org site catalogues an interesting interview conducted with O'Finioan and his friend Dave Corso who, the writer claims, "are both part of Project Talent, an unacknowledged MK-ULTRA military program."

The article continues: "Their joint testimony strongly suggests that the US military has a program of super soldiers, not only those like Duncan (O'Finioan)—with psychic abilities and uncommon strength—but also those in command, who were trained to spot military talent and were skilled in psychotronics, that is: mind control . . .

"Controller and soldier? . . . Their relationship is unclear. But somewhere in the murky waters of the past, two men, from vastly different backgrounds, have come together as friends only to discover that what brings them together may be far more mysterious and sinister than either is prepared to remember."

Since that interview, O'Finioan is on the record as saying an MRI scan he had following a car accident caused a cranial implant to malfunction, removing barriers in his mind that had previously kept memories hidden. He claims those memories leave no doubt that he was a killing machine used for termination assignments and that he was also a victim of MK-Ultra.

O'Finioan's own blog site at duncanofinian.com makes for an interesting read also. In an entry dated January 21, 2014, the man himself posts an open letter from "the survivors of Project Talent" addressed to, among others, President Obama, the US Senate, Congress, the UN and several other organizations. He encourages subscribers to distribute the letter far and wide.

The letter reads: "We, the survivors of MK ULTRA and all of its sub-projects—Project Talent being one of them—are coming to you, the leaders of the free world, for redress. We request immediate action on this matter, as we have waited long enough for our respective governments to take notice of the torture that was illegally and secretly forced upon us as children by the same said governments."

In the same letter, the writers make a number of other requests—including the following: "We ask for acknowledgement of all that was done to us, both as children and adults, by the governments who committed these illegal acts against us, as well as recognition of duties that we performed for our respective countries in the name of freedom and national security . . . And finally, we request that all black projects which use children cease immediately . . . The torture of children can in no way ever be condoned by any country for any reason. It is our highest wish to have a public announcement that these projects using children will be stopped."

The same blog site features an August 2013 OffPlanet Radio interview with one John Stormm, another self-professed survivor of Project Talent and fellow victim of MK-Ultra. He claims he was one of the first batches of *infants* to be inducted into the MK Ultra program.

"I was subjected to torturous physical, mental, genetic, psychological and chemical conditionings, designed to make me into an unstoppable hunter/seeker/assassin," says Stormm. "A master of what the CIA used to refer to as 'the happy accident.' An untraceable stealth weapon capable of fracturing skulls, necks, spines, ribs or whatever and in a split second, leaving a corpse that can be easily set up to appear as a car wreck or household accident that leaves no embarrassing fingers pointed or homicide investigations."

Storm claims that in the late 1960's he was trained and used as a remote viewer in an MK Talent portion of the program, and by 1970, had taken on some of his first combat roles.

Getting back to Governor Jesse Ventura and that *Conspiracy Theory* TV episode, before his director can shout *Cut! It's a wrap!* Ventura informs viewers he's convinced there are more programmed killers out there. "Let's just hope their sites are aimed at the enemy," he says.

Let's hope he's right about that!

Some of America's highest profile assassins—including the likes of John Lennon's killer Mark David Chapman and Robert Kennedy's assassin Sirhan Sirhan—claimed they were CIA-programmed killers hypnotized by MK-Ultra. The media portrayed them as crazed lone gunmen, so naturally the public paid little attention to their claims. Kentbridge, however, knew it was possible some of these men were mind controlled soldiers, or Manchurian Candidates, carrying out assassination orders their conscious minds were not even aware of.

—The Ninth Orphan

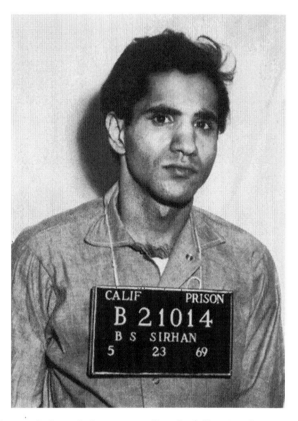

Above: Sirhan Sirhan immediately following his arrest.

*"Sirhan Sirhan" by California Department of Corrections
California Department of Corrections photographic records.
Licensed under Public Domain via Wikimedia Commons*

"RFK MUST DIE"

It seems likely MK-Ultra or a Manchurian Candidate, or possibly both, may have been involved in the 1968 assassination of Robert F. Kennedy, the US Presidential candidate most political analysts agree would have been elected President had he lived.

Our thriller novel *The Orphan Factory* (Sterling Gate Books, 2012) climaxes with a political assassination in the Amazon jungle. Nine and Seventeen, the orphan-operatives charged with carrying out the assassination, tell themselves over and over in their own minds, "Quamina Ezekiel must die." They are not sure why they're repeating this phrase to themselves; the implication is they're under the influence of mind control.

In the writing of that sequence, we include mind control triggers based on alternative theories surrounding some of the most well-known lone gunmen of the 20th Century (including ones obsessed with *The Catcher in the Rye*). But more than any other real-world assassination, this section of our novel was directly inspired by reports of RFK's convicted killer, Sirhan Sirhan.

By all accounts, on the fateful evening of June 5, 1968, the Palestinian-Jordanian assassin appeared to be in a hypnotic state at the scene of the crime—the Ambassador Hotel in Los Angeles. Many believe Sirhan Sirhan was a Manchurian Candidate diligently following instructions his conscious mind was not even aware of.

The prevailing professional opinion is RFK's assassin has never been able to remember *anything* of that night—not entering the hotel, not the killing itself and not leaving the hotel in handcuffs. *Nothing.*

Apparently, Sirhan Sirhan's's only vague memory fragment, if it can be described as that, was said to be a vision of a typewriter he remembered observing all night long as it automatically typed a series of orders for him to follow.

All the evidence at hand seems to indicate Sirhan Sirhan was a brainwashed assassin or, at the very least, he was in a hypnotized state when he pulled the trigger of his .22 caliber revolver.

We refer to his memory blackouts; the reports of multiple witnesses claiming he looked like he was in "a trance"; the psychiatrist who testified at the ensuing court case that Sirhan Sirhan was in a trance state on the night of the crime; and especially the diaries found in his home by the LAPD—diaries whose pages were filled with Sirhan's scribbled handwriting.

Over and over, the words "RFK must die" filled the pages of those diaries. Handwriting analysis indicated the writing was *automatic writing,* meaning Sirhan Sirhan was not conscious of what he was writing.

Another curious fact supporting the hypnotism and mind control theory was that the Jordanian passport-holder had earlier joined the Rosicrucians, an occult group also known as *the Ancient Mystical Order of the Rose Cross.* When several psychiatrists assessed him to be in a hypnotized state after the assassination, Sirhan Sirhan's Rosicrucian membership was treated by many as suspicious, especially as trance and hypnotism are a known part of the group's teachings.

Defence attorney Dr. Bernard Diamond tried to dismiss his client's undeniable hypnotized state by claiming Sirhan Sirhan must have hypnotized himself.

If the assassin was a Manchurian Candidate, the range of suspects could include anyone from the CIA or the Mafia to occultists or the Military Industrial Complex. Many believe the latter to be the culprit, especially as Kennedy had stated he would immediately end the Vietnam War were he to become President.

In a 2011 parole hearing, Sirhan Sirhan's new lawyer, Dr. William Pepper, said his client had been "hypno programmed" and he alluded to the Manchurian Candidate theory.

Ezekiel's head was in the center of the crosshairs of Seventeen's telescopic sight. As she prepared for the shot, the only sound she could hear was Kentbridge's voice in her mind. Her mentor sounded like a broken record. *Quamina Ezekiel must die. Quamina Ezekiel must die. Quamina Ezekiel must die.*

−The Orphan Factory

JOHN LENNON

Another possible victim of a Manchurian Candidate may have been one of *The Beatles*.

Most people old enough remember exactly where they were when they heard the news that John Lennon was shot dead in New York City on December 8, 1980. The murderer was Mark David Chapman—yet another lone gunman who stood glassy-eyed at the crime scene waiting for the police to arrive. A witness to the shooting asked him if he was aware what he'd just done.

"I just shot John Lennon," Chapman calmly replied.

In the court case that followed, Chapman's defence team included psychiatrist Dr. Bernard Diamond. Recognize that name? That's right, he's the very same psychiatrist who assessed Sirhan Sirhan's mental state and, as per his assessment of RFK's assassin, Dr. Diamond stated Chapman was completely insane. Little mention was made of the fact that Chapman was a former World Vision employee who worked as a children's counsellor in refugee camps in Asia and the Middle East.

Author Fenton Bresler put forward the theory in his book *Who Killed John Lennon?* that while Chapman was working in Beirut he fell into the orbit of CIA agents who drugged and brainwashed him as part of the ongoing MK-Ultra program.

What is known is shortly after beginning his charity work in Beirut, Chapman began to exhibit mental illness and was hospitalized as a result. Who he associated with from that point on is not known.

Assuming Chapman was yet another Manchurian Candidate and Lennon wasn't killed randomly, then who on earth would have wanted to kill the peace-loving singer?

Most conspiracy theorists and many researchers point the finger at the US Government for singer-songwriter Lennon was a known threat to the political order of that time. This threat was primarily due to two reasons: his fearless opinions that he gave freely to the press and the sheer size of his following, which was almost unprecedented.

FBI records and other Government files on Lennon indicate the Establishment viewed him as a very dangerous activist. For example, FBI director J. Edgar Hoover personally wrote on Lennon's file: "ALL EXTREMISTS SHOULD BE CONSIDERED DANGEROUS."

Another such file said the ex-Beatle, who by then was a US resident, was able to "draw one million anti-war protestors in any given city in 24 hours." That is some *serious* influence, and judging by the declassified files it's obvious the Military Industrial Complex viewed Lennon as a potential stumbling block to their plans for future wars.

Sean Lennon, the son of John and Yoko, told the *New Yorker* in April 1998 that his father "was dangerous to the government" and "If he had said 'Bomb the White House tomorrow,' there would have been 10,000 people who would have done it. These pacifist

Above: John Lennon Rehearsing "Give Peace a Chance"

"Lie In 15 – John rehearses Give Peace A Chance"
by Roy Kerwood
Photo by Roy Kerwood. Licensed under CC BY 2.5 via
Wikimedia Commons

revolutionaries are historically killed by the government."

The only thing counting against this whole premise is that Lennon was killed in 1980—long after the likes of JFK, RFK, MLK and others were killed and long after the civil unrest of the 1960's and early 1970's had faded. It was a different political and social climate by then with less foreign wars and less volatility within America. Some have even argued that Lennon's star power was waning, at least slightly, by 1980.

Of course, it's not known what Lennon was planning at the time of his death, and for all anyone knows the authorities may have gottenwind of some radical peace movement he was secretly hatching.

To add yet another curiosity to the mix, while Chapman patiently waited for the police to arrive and arrest him, he stood at the scene of the crime reading a copy of *The Catcher in the Rye*. Many conspiracy theorists believe that finding this particular book in the hands of an assassin is no mere coincidence. Regardless, it must have been a macabre sight to see Lennon lying dead on the ground with his murderer standing over him happily reading J.D. Salinger's classic novel.

4

INTRODUCING . . . THE *CATCHER* CRIMINALS

"This is a people shooting hat," I said. "I shoot people in this hat."

–J.D. Salinger, The Catcher in the Rye

The mother of all *Catcher* incidents is probably Mark David Chapman's assassination of John Lennon on December 8, 1980. As widely reported, and as mentioned in the previous chapter, the killer stood over the ex-Beatle's corpse after shooting him and patiently read a copy of Salinger's classic while waiting for police to arrive and arrest him.

Not long before the murder, Chapman had wanted to change his name to the novel's narrator and anti-hero *Holden Caulfield*—so enamored was he with this fictitious character; inside the very copy of the book Chapman had purchased on the day of the murder, police found he'd written, "To Holden Caulfield, From Holden Caulfield, This is my statement"; and during the court case that followed, Chapman read a passage from the novel when addressing the judge and jury during his sentencing.

In the FBI's Vault the following is mentioned under the file *Attempted Assassination of President Ronald Reagan:* "On March 31, 1981, John W. Hinckley, Jr., shot President Ronald Reagan and several others in a failed assassination attempt. The FBI conducted an extensive investigation, named REAGAT."

Just like Mark David Chapman, Hinckley did not attempt to flee the crime site and seemed content to be arrested. After the assassination attempt, which besides wounding President Reagan also left White House Press Secretary James Brady permanently disabled, detectives found a copy of *The Catcher in the Rye* on a coffee table in Hinckley's hotel room.

Above: Hinckley's The attempted assassination of
President Reagan

"Reagan assassination attempt 4."
Licensed under Public Domain via Wikimedia Commons

Before the attempt on Reagan's life, Hinckley had relentlessly stalked actress Jodie Foster for a number of years. He reportedly became obsessed with the Hollywood star after first seeing her in Martin Scorsese's 1976 film *Taxi Driver*. Even to this day, more than three decades later, Foster has hardly ever spoken of the incident and has been known to walk out of interviews when Hinckley's name, or the Reagan assassination attempt, is mentioned.

The shooter, whose full name was John Warnock Hinckley Jr., tried to assassinate Reagan because he said he thought that would impress Jodie Foster. It was later revealed that during his stay in the Washington D.C. psychiatric hospital St. Elizabeths, Hinckley had exchanged letters with serial killer Ted Bundy and sought the address of mass murderer Charles Manson.

Another *Catcher* fan was Robert John Bardo, yet another three-name assassin, who murdered American actress and model Rebecca Schaeffer on July 18, 1989. Like Mark David Chapman, Bardo was carrying a copy of Salinger's book on him at the scene of the crime.

The one-time stalker of Madonna and child actress Samantha Smith, Bardo stalked Schaeffer before finding her alone at her home in Los Angeles. He shot the star of *My Sister Sam* TV series in the chest then threw his red paperback copy of the book onto the roof of a nearby building as he fled.

As for JFK's killer Lee Harvey Oswald, *The Catcher in the Rye* was found in a raid on his Dallas, Texas apartment after the assassination. His other books included George Orwell's *Animal Farm* and Adolf Hitler's *Mein Kampf*. Although unconfirmed, it has been claimed by a few sources that Oswald was very keen on Salinger's novel, which apparently was his favorite.

Criminals not officially acknowledged but rumored in conspiracy circles to have been directly influenced by *Catcher* include RFK's assassin Sirhan Sirhan, Lee Harvey Oswald's killer Jack Ruby, Martin Luther King's murderer James Earl Ray, cult leader and killer Charles Manson, the Washington Sniper John Allen Muhammad, Jonestown founder Jim Jones, the Boston Strangler Albert DeSalvo, the unidentified Zodiac Killer, the Unabomber Ted Kaczynski, serial killer Ted Bundy and the Oklahoma bomber Timothy McVeigh.

Even if none of these killers (listed directly above) were inspired by Salinger's novel, the list of murderers and other criminals whose possession of, or obsession with, the book that has been proven is surprisingly lengthy and throws up a thousand unanswered questions.

Isn't it also possible, probable or even highly likely other criminals have been inspired by *The Catcher in the Rye?* How many assassins disposed of their copies after committing murders or other crimes—as Robert John Bardo tried to do? Maybe others were as obsessed with the book as Mark David Chapman was, but subsequent investigations failed to uncover those details? After all, not every criminal keeps a diary or records of their personal library of reading material.

As one book reviewer wrote on Amazon.com in a review of Salinger's classic: "There may be countless other criminals and stalkers who have identified with the book's main character, Holden Caulfield."

"A substitute teacher out on Long Island was dropped from his job for fighting with a student. A few weeks later, he returned to the classroom, shot the student, unsuccessfully, held the class hostage and then shot himself. Successfully. This fact caught my eye: last sentence, *Times;* A neighbor described him as a nice boy—always reading Catcher in the Rye. The nitwit, Chapman, who shot John Lennon said he did it because he wanted to draw the attention of the world to The Catcher in the Rye and the reading of the book would be his defense. And young Hinckley, the whiz kid who shot Reagan and his press secretary, said if you want my defense all you have to do is read Catcher in the Rye."

–Monologue delivered by Will Smith in the film Six Degrees of Separation (1993)

5

A LITERARY PSY-OP?

Minutes earlier, Naylor had hypnotized Seventeen using the MK-Ultra voice commands he'd recently received from Langley. For years, he'd wanted to have his way with Seventeen. Receiving the orphans' MK-Ultra codes had presented him with the perfect opportunity. It was perfect because she would never remember a thing. The copy of *The Catcher in the Rye* he'd given her was all part of the mind control program. The book acted as an additional control mechanism to activate hypnotism triggers in the brain.

–The Ninth Orphan

In our thriller novel *The Ninth Orphan* (2012, Sterling Gate Books), Nine and his fellow orphans have a triggering device which happens to be the names of all the planets in the solar system—Mercury, Venus, Earth, Mars, Jupiter, Saturn, Uranus, Neptune, Pluto. When the orphans hear or read those words in precisely that order, they immediately fall into a hypnotized state as a result of their MK-Ultra programming. That's all their handlers have to do to gain total control of their charges and force them to do *anything,* even kill.

This phrasing technique we included in our novel was based on declassified CIA documents, as well as published research on hypnotism, revealing how mind control has been shown to work. It's only one of many techniques used, but one that crops up again and again in the documented evidence of successful mind control experiments.

Accepting for a moment that *Catcher* is such a triggering device, it would likely set off MK-Ultra subjects by having carefully phrased words in strategic parts of the book. Nobody outside of the sleeper assassins and their intelligence agency handlers would be able to recognize such phrases as being abnormal, especially if crafted by such a skillful writer as Salinger.

Above: One of the other main Catcher covers

(photo credit: public domain)

Richard Condon's 1959 classic novel *The Manchurian Candidate* uses only one card, the Queen of Hearts, out of an entire deck of cards as a triggering device for activating the mind control programs in the story's main characters. If the mind controlled subjects are shown a deck of cards, card by card, they're hypnotized simply because the Queen of Hearts happens to be in the deck. Keep in mind there are 52 cards in a deck, so about 98% of cards in the deck aren't related to the mind control program at all.

Similarly, 98% of Salinger's book would simply be literature and probably have nothing to do with nefarious intelligence agency programs like MK-Ultra. It wouldn't have upset the flow of the novel if Salinger, or perhaps his publishing house editor, had inserted a few brief triggering devices, or phrases, at the behest of the CIA or FBI or other such agency.

"It's funny. All you have to do is say something nobody understands and they'll do practically anything you want them to."

–J.D. Salinger, The Catcher in the Rye

If the novel contains mind control triggers there are two obvious possibilities regarding exactly who inserted them.

One is that Salinger didn't deliberately insert such triggers in *Catcher* and had no knowledge his novel would be used for mind control. Instead, the book was simply used by intelligence agencies, without his permission, as a triggering device to prompt chosen subjects to kill. This would likely have been achieved during the brainwashing process of subjects by repeating certain sentences from the book over and over. It may also be true that the likes of the CIA simply selected the novel as the perfect story to brainwash lone gunmen given its themes of alienation and angst.

The second possibility is that Salinger knowingly inserted mind control phrases into the novel and worked in collusion with high ranking officials in the US intelligence community. Following this theme Salinger along with his advisors, or controllers perhaps, planted excerpts of neurolinguistic writing designed to *speak* to an assassin's brain.

How could any ordinary writer achieve that? Such a question assumes Salinger was an ordinary writer . . .

"Don't ever tell anybody anything. If you do, you start missing everybody."

–J.D. Salinger, The Catcher in the Rye

6

THE AUTHOR'S SECRETIVE LIFE

"Anyway, I'm sort of glad they've got the atomic bomb invented. If there's ever another war, I'm going to sit right the hell on top of it. I'll volunteer for it, I swear to God I will."

–J.D. Salinger, The Catcher in the Rye

J.D. Salinger was by all accounts a recluse and, of all the 20th Century's masters of literature, he's probably the one least is known about. This is due in part to his extreme desire for privacy. A good example of this was the reported act of painting his forest cabin in camouflage colors so nobody could find him!

Despite living until 2010, some 59 years after *The Catcher in the Rye* was first published and became a phenomenal worldwide bestseller, he never published another novel.

Salinger's last published work, the short story collection *Hapworth 16, 1924,* came out in 1965. From that point on he continued to write, but his writing remained for his eyes only. Calls from his millions of fans eager to read more of his works apparently fell on deaf ears.

Besides being reclusive, many have labeled him eccentric and even mean-spirited. There are numerous colorful stories about him. These include him regularly drinking his own urine, becoming enraged whenever his infant children cried, being a hypochondriac, telling one of his wives never to disturb him "unless the house is burning down," exploring Dianetics (later renamed Scientology) and meeting its founder L. Ron Hubbard, and having his photo removed from all his books' jackets.

However, what many conspiracy theorists believe holds the key in the whole mystery surrounding *Catcher* is Salinger's life before he wrote the book. During and immediately after WW2 to be precise.

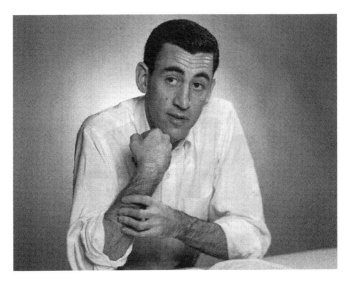

Above: A rare photograph of J.D. Salinger

(photo credit: public domain)

And like many other instances of mind control operations conducted in the United States over the years, the controversies linked to Salinger's masterpiece appear to lead directly back to the Nazis.

What few of Salinger's fans ever fully comprehend is the man's extensive military and intelligence employment history. Employment that included working for the OSS—the forerunner to the CIA—on highly classified projects in Europe post-WW2.

According to the 1988 unauthorized biography *In Search of J.D. Salinger,* by Ian Hamilton, Salinger worked for the Defense Intelligence during WW2 and served with the Counter Intelligence Corps. His main duties, Hamilton wrote, involved interrogating captured Nazis.

And on September 3, 2013, *The Telegraph* ran an article headlined *JD Salinger's five unpublished titles revealed, and how Second World War shaped his thinking.* According to the article, one of Salinger's unpublished books is "about his time interrogating prisoners of war when he served working in the counter-intelligence division." That book, incidentally, has the revealing title, *A Counterintelligence Agent's Diary.*

Equally intriguing is another unpublished Salinger book titled *A World War II Love Story*, which the same article claims is "based on his brief marriage to Sylvia, a Nazi collaborator, just after the war."

Ian Hamilton's *In Search of J.D. Salinger* also mentions that as the war came to a close Salinger was an active participant in the "deNazification of Germany."

Now let's think about that word for a moment . . . *deNazification*.

That word could very well mean Salinger was actively involved in the genesis of *Project Paperclip,* that clandestine program we detailed in chapter 2, which involved smuggling hundreds of Nazis into America and using them to progress the US intelligence and scientific sectors. After all, declassified files have since revealed that much of America's (and the Soviet Union's) efforts in deNazifying Europe in truth amounted to gathering up all the Nazi regime's incredible scientific technologies, not to mention its scientists.

In fact, some researchers have gone as far as saying the process was more of a *reNazification* than a deNazification. Or, put another way, fascism continued, stronger than ever, but in another form and leaping across oceans to far-away countries like America.

As we've shown in earlier chapters through declassified documents and mainstream media reports, some of the *Paperclip Nazi* scientists squirreled into the US after WW2 were charged with developing America's earliest attempts at mind control. This was due to the fact that the Nazis had made tremendous progress in the science of the mind—primarily because of the horrific experiments they conducted on *live* prisoners during the Holocaust.

Declassified documents also prove these Americanized Nazis had a major influence on the intelligence community in the West post-WW2, especially with US mind control programs which had fascist science written all over them.

Given Salinger's top-secret wartime experiences, some conspiracy theorists have connected the dots. They assert that he planted mind control triggers in *The Catcher in the Rye* using the advanced knowledge he was exposed to in his dealings with Nazi scientists. This theory suggests the book was written in such a way that it could be used in MK-Ultra and the CIA's earlier mind control projects such as *Project Artichoke*.

These are wild theories indeed. However, given what we now know (and are still learning) about how advanced Nazi mind technologies were, and how much they shaped the modern US intelligence community, these theories should not be wholly dismissed.

Whatever the case, the actual reason for Salinger's reclusiveness may have been because of what he knew, or what he had been forced to do, in this so-called deNazification process after WW2. This idea is potentially supported by Hamilton's biography, which argues that Salinger had post-traumatic stress disorder due to wartime activities that left him a forever disturbed individual.

To shed more light on Salinger's underreported work for the mysterious Counter Intelligence Corps (CIC), the Wikimedia footnote for the above image is perhaps helpful:

"America's Secret Army by Ian Sayer and Douglas Botting—Franklin Watts New York / Toronto 1989 tells the story of the Counter Intelligence Corps (CIC). Established in World War I when the CIC was called the Corps of Intelligence Police (CIP) the Corps was greatly expanded in World War II but never had more than 5000 personnel. Many agents would travel with combat units. CIC Agents took basic

Above: America's Secret Army reveals Salinger
was an elite CIC Agent.

*"Bud Uanna Counter Intelligence Corps Americas Secret
Army p.2" by CIC777 – Own work.
Licensed under CC BY-SA 3.0 via Wikimedia Commons*

training with combat troops and CIC training at Fort Holabird, Maryland. Agents learned many technical skills and Jujitsu. Some agents trained at the advanced school in Chicago, Illinois which gave them classification of Special Agents. Bud Uanna wrote a manual used by CIC Agents and taught at the CIC school in Chicago before being selected for Counter Intelligence and Security duties with the Manhattan Project. CIC agents were known for their self confidence, inquisitiveness, adaptability and timing. *J. D. Salinger the author of "The Catcher in the Rye" was a CIC Agent in Europe.* All had above average IQ's. Bud Uanna took 2 IQ tests scoring 160 on one and 180 on the other. Agents were never to divulge the existence of the CIC to anyone outside of the Army and although many of them were enlisted men they were not required to give their rank to officers under the rank of General. *They were unknown to the American public and a puzzle to many in the U.S. Army.* On the other hand the Office of Strategic Services (OSS) got the publicity. As perceived by the CIC the OSS, also known as "Oh So Social" because of the large number of society types in its ranks were "befuddled amateurs with an inexhaustible supply of funds and an air of mysticism" who claimed the credit for CIC achievements. Shown on the left side are Bud Uanna's CIC Association and Military Intelligence Association Membership cards for 1961—the year he died."

Seventeen frowned when she noticed the top button of her blouse was undone. Her gaze strayed to the copy of *The Catcher in the Rye* on her lap. The orphan had no recollection of picking up the book at any stage. In fact, she'd never even read it. All she knew about the novel was it had been found on the men behind the assassination and attempted assassination of John Lennon and Ronald Reagan respectively, and its author, J.D. Salinger, had significant ties to the CIA.

–The Ninth Orphan

7

MORE ON THE MAN WHO KILLED
JOHN LENNON

On February 9, 1981, *The New York Times* ran an article stating Mark David Chapman was preparing to plead insanity at the upcoming trial in which he was accused of murdering John Lennon. The article mentions Chapman had developed an unhealthy "obsession" with *Catcher* and "in a handwritten statement delivered to The New York Times last week, Mr. Chapman" had "urged everyone to read the novel, a copy of which was in his possession when he was arrested."

Chapman had apparently told the NY Times that reading the book would "help many to understand what has happened."

The newspaper also reported that the accused's statement ended with: "My wish is for all of you to someday read 'The Catcher in the Rye.' All of my efforts will now be devoted toward this goal, for this extraordinary book holds many answers. My true hope is that in wanting to find these answers you will read 'The Catcher in the Rye.' Thank you."

The accused's statement was signed "Mark David Chapman—The Catcher in the Rye."

During the trial that followed, Chapman continued to promote the book. At times he would open up a copy and begin reading intently for all to see the book's cover. On other occasions he would stand up excitedly and shout to everyone in the court, imploring them to read the novel.

"If you sat around there long enough and heard all the phonies applauding and all, you got to hate everybody in the world."

–J.D. Salinger, The Catcher in the Rye

It also came out during the court case that shortly before the assassination Chapman would sit in his room chanting the mantra, "THE PHONY MUST DIE SAYS THE CATCHER IN THE RYE!" as well as "JOHN LENNON MUST DIE SAYS THE CATCHER IN THE RYE!"

These phrases are eerily similar to Sirhan Sirhan's documented diary entries in which he repeatedly wrote "RFK MUST DIE!"

Another parallel is that the word *phony* in the aforementioned mantra was borrowed from *Catcher,* once again indicating that Chapman's murder of Lennon was somehow inspired by the book.

There is also an urban legend which says John Lennon himself was in the middle of reading the novel the week he was killed. There's no solid evidence to confirm this, and if Yoko Ono knows, she isn't saying.

What can be confirmed is Mark David Chapman's ties with World Vision. As mentioned in chapter 3, it's a little known fact that Chapman was a former World Vision employee and children's counsellor who worked in refugee camps all over the world. Contrary to media reports, he was by all accounts formerly

Above: Yoko Ono delivering flowers to
John Lennon's memorial

"Yoko Ono 2005" by Hamletphase
Licensed under CC BY 2.0 via Wikimedia Commons

a good citizen who exhibited no signs of mental illness.

As some researchers have speculated, Chapman may have been drugged by CIA agents and forced into their MK-Ultra program while doing aid work for World Vision in Beirut. Some conspiracy theories claim this MK-Ultra program included setting up mind control triggers by repeating certain sentences from *Catcher* for long, sustained periods.

But that's not where the World Vision link to Salinger's novel, or its deadly aftermath, ends . . .

8

THE HINCKLEY-BUSH-REAGAN CONNECTION

"I'm the most terrific liar you ever saw in your life."

—J.D. Salinger, The Catcher in the Rye

Surprisingly, World Vision crops up again with Reagan's attempted assassin, John Hinckley, Jr., whose father, John Warnock Hinckley, Sr., was president of World Vision United States.

The gunman's father was also a multi-millionaire Texas oilman and President and Chairman of the independent oil and gas exploration firm Vanderbilt Energy Corporation. Considering he belonged to such a wealthy and prominent family, it seems rather odd that John Hinckley, Jr. was always portrayed by the media as some kind of vagabond who did nothing but stalk Jodie Foster and read *Catcher* all day.

What was also rarely if ever reported was that Hinckley Sr. was a major financial contributor to the failed 1980 Presidential campaign of the Vice President, George H. W. Bush, the man who would have become President sooner had Reagan been killed in the assassination attempt.

But the Bush-Hinckley family ties don't end there. Oh no, not by a long shot . . .

Hinckley's older brother, Scott, had a dinner date scheduled at the home of Neil Bush, the Vice President's son, the day after the assassination attempt on Reagan. A March 31, 1981 news headline by Associated Press confirmed this: *Bush Son Had Dinner Plans With Hinckley Brother Before Shooting*.

George H.W. Bush's other son, George W. Bush, also admitted to journalists that he may have had dealings with Scott Hinckley who was Vice-President of Vanderbilt Energy, but could not remember either way.

Obviously this is all very circumstantial, but then again . . . What are the odds that the family of the convicted shooter of the President were intimately tied to the Vice President's family and were also Texas oil tycoons who part-financed the Vice President's unsuccessful presidential campaign against the President?

And why were so few of these facts ever reported by the mainstream media?

Some conspiracy theorists have asked if John Warnock Hinckley Jr.'s actions mirror the plot of Richard Condon's *The Manchurian Candidate?* And if so, was *The Catcher in the Rye* used to transmit the appropriate assassination triggers?

In the book *George Bush: The Unauthorized Biography,* published in 2004 by Progressive Press, Webster Griffin Tarpley and Anton Chaitkin imply that at least the former may have been the case.

Tarpley and Chaitkin state, "For Bush, the vice presidency was not an end in itself, but merely another stage in the ascent towards the pinnacle of the federal bureaucracy, the White

Above: George H. W. Bush as Vice President

*"George H. W. Bush, President of the United States,
official portrait" by Library of Congress
Licensed under Public Domain via Wikimedia Commons*

House. With the help of his Brown Brothers, Harriman/Skull and Bones network, Bush had now reached the point where but a single human life stood between him and the presidency . . . In the midst of the Bush-Baker cabal's relentless drive to seize control over the Reagan administration, John Warnock Hinckley Jr. carried out his attempt to assassinate President Reagan."

The writers continue by asking whether Hinckley was "part of a conspiracy, domestic or international? Not more than five hours after the attempt to kill Reagan, on the basis of the most fragmentary early reports, before Hinckley had been properly questioned, and before a full investigation had been carried out, a group of cabinet officers chaired by George Bush had ruled out a priori any conspiracy."

And ever since, all levels of the US Government, from the White House and FBI down, have maintained that there was no conspiracy involved in the assassination attempt on President Reagan.

When one journalist put all these seemingly connected events to the White House, Bush spokeswoman Shirley M. Green replied on March 31, 1981 that it was all just "Bizarre happenstance, a weird coincidence."

It's also worth noting that none of the Bush family, not the Vice President or Neil Bush or George W. Bush, was ever questioned by the FBI regarding their string of connections with the Hinckley family. If a formal FBI investigation was conducted, you would assume interviewing Vice President Bush and his sons would have been a logical starting point.

Maybe the eighth grade pupil at Alice Deal Junior High School, in Washington D.C., accurately summarized the assassination attempt best when responding to a task set all the students the day after the assassination attempt. Asked to express their views on the incident, the pupil told teachers, "It is a plot by Vice President Bush to get into power. If Bush becomes President, the CIA would be in charge of the country."

Perhaps the young Hinckley also accurately summarized the whole incident. Scribbled notes found in his cell during a random search described a political conspiracy involving either the Left or the Right and orchestrated to attempt to assassinate the President. Unfortunately, this potential evidence was never brought up in the court case.

Above: John Hinckley, Jr. Mugshot

*"John Hinckley Jr. FBI Mugshot" by FBI
Licensed under Public Domain via Wikimedia Commons*

Reporting on the trial, the media fixated on three points: Hinckley's stalking of Jodie Foster, the defense team's promotion of the *insanity* argument, and the fact that the first thing detectives saw when they busted in to Hinckley's hotel room after the shooting was his copy of *The Catcher in the Rye*.

9

FORMERLY BANNED, NOW
REQUIRED READING

These days, *Catcher* is 'required reading' in most high school English courses in the US and throughout much of the Western world. This despite the fact it has been banned by various schools and libraries, and criticized by numerous parent and teacher groups as being immoral literature due to its use of profanity and themes of excessive rebellion and alienation.

The fact it's now required reading has inspired some conspiracy theorists—most probably of the Tinfoil Hat variety—to envisage a grand conspiracy in which mind control is being conducted on a mass scale in order to corrupt, pacify or otherwise control today's youth.

Reclusive *Guns N' Roses* lead singer Axl Rose took part in an online chat on December 12, 2008 on the GNR fan community site. When a fan asked him about a song he'd written called *Catcher N' The Rye* on GNR's new album *Chinese Democracy,* Axl's responses seem to indicate he believed the theory that the novel can incite violent acts when read by certain individuals.

"For me," he said, "the song is inspired by what's referred to sometimes as Holden Caulfield Syndrome . . . I feel there's a possibility that how the writing is structured with the thinking of the main character could somehow re-program, for lack of a better word, some who may be a bit more vulnerable, with a skewed way of thinking."

Axl also mentioned he felt that the novel is "utter garbage" and said he agrees "wholeheartedly that it should be discontinued as required reading in schools."

Above: Axl Rose not a fan of The Catcher.

"Axl rose in israel" by Original uploader was אל י באבא *Licensed under CC BY-SA 3.0 via Wikimedia Commons*

10

THE ARGUMENT AGAINST THE
CATCHER CONSPIRACY

"They say music can alter moods and talk to you / Well, can it load a gun up for you and cock it too? / Well if it can, and the next time you assault a dude / Just tell the judge it was my fault, and I'll get sued."

–*Eminem, lyric from Sing for the Moment*

We concede that we and others may be reading too much into the murders that some connect with Salinger's classic novel. It could be argued that, at best, those murders are only loosely related to *Catcher* for it was, after all, a critically acclaimed masterpiece and one of the biggest selling books of the 20th Century.

Given its worldwide popularity, the fact that the book was found in the possession of a few killers—a handful at most—could just be pure coincidence.

Today, if some new Presidential assassin or serial killer had a copy of *The Da Vinci Code* or a *Harry Potter* book in their possession, would anyone blink? And even though religious books such as the Bible, the Qur'an (Koran) and the Torah have inspired innumerable assassins, madmen and terrorists—some well known, some not—surely that doesn't mean there are insidious mind control programs infused in their writings?

What about Mark David Chapman? we hear you ask.

Yes, the man was completely obsessed with the book, but then again so, too, were countless other (normal) young people around the world in the decades following its publication. Many commented they felt as if Holden Caulfield was voicing their own inner reality and the angers and frustrations they felt in their own lives. And for those who are insane, as Chapman appeared to end up, a work as brilliantly and intensely written as Salinger's novel was bound to reach the darkest corners of their brains, encouraging those individuals to take the story too literally, or out of context, or both.

People who are mentally ill often obsess over all kinds of artworks—such as Michael Jackson's music, Stanley Kubrick's movies or Andy Warhol's paintings—believing there are dark messages embedded in those works, instructing them to kill. It's simply a case of criminal minds latching on to warped ideas and dark concepts in popular culture. And certainly *Catcher* is not the only novel to inspire murders, and it won't be the last.

As Aidan Doyle wrote on December 16, 2003 in a Salon.com article entitled *When books kill:* "A copy of 'The Turner Diaries' was found in Timothy McVeigh's car when he was arrested. The novel was written by a leader of the National Alliance and tells the story of a white supremacist group that overthrows the government and subsequently eradicates nonwhites as well as race traitors. The narrator destroys FBI headquarters by detonating a truck loaded with ammonium nitrate and fuel oil. McVeigh used a similar mechanism to destroy the federal building in Oklahoma City, killing 168 people."

The same article also mentions it's not just books that have inspired killings. "A $246 million lawsuit was lodged against the makers of the game *Grand Theft Auto III* by the families of two people shot by teenagers allegedly inspired by the game. Such movies as 'Natural Born Killers,' 'A Clockwork Orange' and 'Money Train' have routinely been accused of inspiring copycat crimes."

It has been estimated more than 100,000,000 people have read *Catcher*. With only a few crazy incidents attributed to it, you could reasonably argue this is not a bad record and certainly isn't enough to justify outlandish conspiracy theories.

Above: Torrey DeVitto (star of The Vampire Diaries)
reading the book.

*"Vampire Diaries 12 (7290480306)" by GabboT – Vampire
Diaries 12. Uploaded by stemoc. Licensed under CC BY-SA 2.0
via Wikimedia Commons*

Connecting the Dots . . .

As mentioned, the alleged conspiracy surrounding *The Catcher in the Rye* has already been studied ad nauseam and the general consensus by experts is that it is a mere coincidence that these criminals committed such horrific crimes after reading the book.

But how many of the so-called experts know about MK-Ultra and the highly documented history of mind control? And how many are aware of the intelligence community's experiments proving Manchurian Candidates are indeed possible?

We're certainly not implying we are experts, but it's a fact that most who have analyzed *Catcher* conspiracy theories have been authorities in either literature or criminology with highly specific knowledge in their chosen fields. Perhaps to more accurately assess this subject a prerequisite would be to have a broader knowledge of such topics as the way intelligence agencies operate, the dark history of assassinations and suspicious lone gunmen, and Project Paperclip's Americanized Nazis as well as understanding how advanced the science of mind control really is.

We ain't saying *Catcher* is definitely a mind control mechanism for those who have been brainwashed by intelligence agencies. But at the very least, the book had an accidental and unintended influence on some of the most heinous and high profile crimes of the 20th Century. And to us that seems very convenient or coincidental or suspicious—take your pick.

Just like any good story, maybe there's a few facts hidden within the fiction and a healthy dose of fiction buried amongst the facts. Perhaps J.D. Salinger never bothered to publicly comment on the crimes associated with his book as he liked the mystery that surrounded it.

And on that note let's allow the man himself have the final word . . .

"It's partly true, too, but it isn't all true," Salinger wrote in *The Catcher in the Rye*. "People always think something's all true."

THE END

If you liked this book, the authors would greatly appreciate a review from you on Amazon.

OTHER BOOKS

BY JAMES & LANCE MORCAN
PUBLISHED BY STERLING GATE BOOKS

NON-FICTION:

DEBUNKING HOLOCAUST DENIAL THEORIES: Two Non-Jews Affirm the Historicity of the Nazi Genocide

THE ORPHAN CONSPIRACIES: 29 Conspiracy Theories from The Orphan Trilogy

GENIUS INTELLIGENCE: Secret Techniques and Technologies to Increase IQ (The Underground Knowledge Series, #1)

ANTIGRAVITY PROPULSION: Human or Alien Technologies? (The Underground Knowledge Series, #2)

MEDICAL INDUSTRIAL COMPLEX: The $ickness Industry, Big Pharma and Suppressed Cures (The Underground Knowledge Series, #3)

THE CATCHER IN THE RYE ENIGMA: J.D. Salinger's Mind Control Triggering Device or a Coincidental Literary Obsession of Criminals? (The Underground Knowledge Series, #4)

INTERNATIONAL BANKSTER$: The Global Banking Elite Exposed and the Case for Restructuring Capitalism (The Underground Knowledge Series, #5)

BANKRUPTING THE THIRD WORLD: How the Global Elite Drown Poor Nations in a Sea of Debt (The Underground Knowledge Series, #6)

UNDERGROUND BASES: Subterranean Military Facilities and the Cities Beneath Our Feet (The Underground Knowledge Series, #7)

HISTORICAL FICTION:

Into the Americas (A novel based on a true story)

World Odyssey (The World Duology, #1)

Fiji: A Novel (The World Duology, #2)

White Spirit (A novel based on a true story)

THRILLERS:

The Ninth Orphan (The Orphan Trilogy, #1)

The Orphan Factory (The Orphan Trilogy, #2)

The Orphan Uprising (The Orphan Trilogy, #3)

21573613R00072

Printed in Great Britain
by Amazon